NATURAL DISASTERS

TSUNAMIS

Luke Thompson

HIGH
interest
books

Children's Press
A Division of Grolier Publishing
New York / London / Hong Kong / Sydney
Danbury, Connecticut

Book Design: MaryJane Wojciechowski
Contributing Editors: Jennifer Ceaser and Rob Kirkpatrick

Photo Credits: Cover © Ron Sanford/International Stock; pp. 4, 5 © Christophe
Loviny; p. 7 © Douglas Peebles/International Stock; pp. 8, 9 © Corbis; p. 15 ©
Roger Ressmeyer/Corbis; p. 17 © Index Stock Imagery; pp. 18, 19 © Roy
Corral/Corbis; p. 21 © NOAA; pp. 27, 28, 30, 31 © Associated Press AP/AP
Wide World Photos; p. 32 © Associated Press/NOAA/AP Wide World Photos;
p. 35 © Photo Disk; p. 36 © Michael S. Yamashita/Corbis; p. 39 © Warren
Faidley/International Stock

Visit Children's Press on the Internet at:
http://publishing.grolier.com

Library of Congress Cataloging-in-Publication Data

Thompson, Luke.
    Tsunamis / by Luke Thompson.
       p. cm. – (Natural disasters)
    Includes bibliographical references and index.
    Summary: Defines tsunamis and describes the geologic forces that cause
       them, as well as the damage they can inflict when the huge walls of
       ocean water strike land.
    ISBN 0-516-23368-8 (lib. bdg.) – ISBN 0-516-23568-0 (pbk.)
    1. Tsunamis—Juvenile literature. [1. Tsunamis.] I. Title.

GC221.5.T48 2000
551.47'024—dc21

                                                    00-024370

CONTENTS

*An earthquake hit Mindoro Island in the Philippines on November 15, 1994. Three minutes later, the earthquake produced a giant ocean wave almost 20 feet (6 m) high. The wave, called a tsunami (soo-**nah**-mee), hit 25 miles (40 km) along the northern and eastern shores of Mindoro. Then it surged on to the state of Baco.*

In Baco, the tsunami smashed into the shore and drowned forty-one people. Residents reported hearing a sound like the loud gush of a strong rain as the wave hit the coast. Then the tsunami moved on to Calapan, the Philippine capital. There, the tsunami drowned seventeen people. More than half of the victims were children under the age of ten.

In all, 1,500 houses were washed away and more than 7,500 homes were

This is a view of Mindoro Island before the tsunami of 1994 struck.

damaged. The tsunami also washed away twenty-four bridges, cutting off many towns and villages. More than seventy-eight people in the Philippines lost their lives in the killer tsunami.

Tsunamis do not occur as often as do other natural disasters, such as earthquakes or tornadoes. Yet tsunamis can be just as destructive and deadly. They can strike quickly and without warning. Their effects on land and on people can be devastating. Many times, people drown in tsunami waters before they can even think about running for safety.

Tsunami waves can be as destructive as earthquakes or tornadoes.

CHAPTER ONE

HOW A TSUNAMI STARTS

On December 12, 1992, a large earthquake struck just off the shore of Flores Island, Indonesia. Five minutes after the quake, several large tsunami waves hit the northern shore of the island. In the town of Wuring, the waves destroyed most of the houses and drowned eighty-seven people. The tsunami moved on to the small village of Riang-Kroko. Of the 406 people living in the town, 137 lost their lives to the deadly waves.

Then the tsunami crashed into Babi Island, 24 miles (40 km) away. Of the island's 1,093 citizens, 263 were killed. In all, the 1992 tsunami killed 1,690 people and destroyed 18,000 houses.

A tsunami in Indonesia destroyed towns and drowned thousands of people.

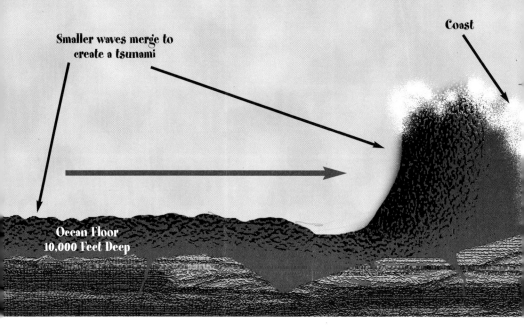

Smaller waves merge to
create a tsunami

Coast

Ocean Floor
10,000 Feet Deep

This illustration shows how a tsunami forms.

A tsunami starts as a group of large ocean waves caused by sudden movements deep in the ocean floor. These waves merge into one giant wave as the tsunami gets closer to the shore. Tsunami waves are much larger and much faster than are normal ocean waves. If you were to see a tsunami, it would look like a huge wall of water crashing toward you. Tsunami waves can grow to more than 100 feet (30.5 m) high. They can travel at speeds up to 600 miles (966 km) per hour across the ocean.

WHAT IS A TSUNAMI?

A tsunami often is confused with a tidal wave. Actually, they are two completely different natural events. Tidal waves are caused by ocean tides. The moon affects ocean tides by pulling on Earth with a force called gravity.

Only sudden movements in the ocean cause tsunamis. Earthquakes, volcanoes, and landslides are events that create these movements.

EARTHQUAKES

The surface of Earth is made of a layer of solid rock. This layer is called the crust. Earth's crust is broken into nine larger—and at least twelve smaller—slabs of rock called tectonic plates. These tectonic plates move against each other. Over time, pressure begins to build between plates. The stress on the plates becomes so great that Earth needs a way to release the pressure. This release comes in the form of a sudden break in the crust.

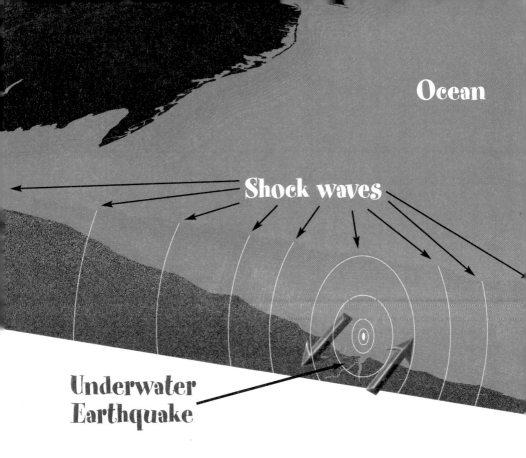

Ocean

Shock waves

Underwater
Earthquake

Shock waves given off by an underwater earthquake can cause huge waves.

When the crust breaks suddenly, the movement produces seismic (shock) waves. Seismic waves cause the earth to vibrate. This is what we call an earthquake. The shock waves of large earthquakes are very powerful. Seismic waves begin at the starting point of an earthquake—the epicenter. Seismic waves travel outward from the epicenter in a circular motion. They can travel as fast as 100 miles (161 km) in a matter of a few seconds.

DID YOU KNOW?

The Japanese coined the word tsunami. It was made from two Japanese words: *tsu*, which means harbor, and *nami*, which means wave.

When an earthquake happens in the ocean floor, seismic waves create a swell (large surge) of water. The swell ripples outward to create sea waves. These waves travel away from the quake's epicenter in all directions.

Tsunami waves, also called seismic sea waves, are very strong. If a tsunami begins near land, the waves can cause almost immediate destruction. Tsunami waves also can cause damage on land hundreds of miles away from an earthquake's epicenter.

VOLCANOES

Volcanoes are places in the crust where magma (boiling rock) and hot gas rise to Earth's surface. When too much magma and gas collect underneath a volcano, they push to get to the surface. The volcano explodes and releases the magma and gas. This event is called an eruption.

Volcanoes are found both on land and under water. When a volcano under or near the ocean erupts, shock waves surge through the water. If the shock waves are very powerful, they can produce tsunami waves.

"KRAK" AND BOOM!

Although earthquakes cause 95 percent of tsunamis, it was a volcano that caused the world's worst tsunami. In 1883, a volcano on Krakatoa in the South Pacific erupted. The explosion sent huge waves surging toward the islands of Java and Sumatra. Waves got as high as 115 feet (35 m). More than 36,000 people drowned on the two islands.

A diver investigates an underwater volcano.

LANDSLIDES

Tsunamis can occur when huge rocks or large chunks of land slide into the ocean. This event is called a landslide. In 1958, an earthquake created a landslide that poured into Alaska's Lituya Bay. The landslide created a tsunami that pushed across the bay and crashed high onto the shore. The waves wiped out trees that were 1,700 feet (516 m) up the hillside.

WHERE TSUNAMIS OCCUR

Most tsunamis occur in the Pacific Ocean. This is because many earthquakes and volcanic eruptions happen in the Pacific region. Most earthquakes occur where tectonic plates meet. Many of these plates meet in the Pacific Ocean. A lot of volcanic activity also occurs in this ocean. The region has been nicknamed the Ring of Fire because of the large circle of underwater volcanoes.

Most tsunamis occur in the Pacific Ocean.

CHAPTER TWO

HOW TSUNAMIS MOVE

The earthquakes that strike Alaska are some of the strongest earthquakes on Earth. The state also is surrounded by water on three sides. This combination can make for huge and deadly tsunamis.

On the evening of March 27, 1964, two days before Easter Sunday, the Good Friday earthquake struck. It hit southern Alaska near the city of Anchorage. As the shock waves died down, a local tsunami from Prince William Sound headed straight for the mainland.

The Chena, a large cargo ship, was docked at the port town of Valdez when the tsunami hit. People had come to the dock to watch the ship unload. The tsunami struck the ship and turned it on its side. The captain later said: "I saw people running—with no place to run to. They were just engulfed by buildings, water,

This is the port town of Valdez where the Good Friday tsunami hit in 1964.

19

mud, and everything. The Chena raised about 30 feet (9 m) on an oncoming wave. The whole ship lifted and turned to its side about 50 degrees. Then it was slammed down heavily on the spot where the docks had disintegrated [been broken apart] moments before."

The tsunami crashed inland, killing 110 Alaskans. The earthquake and tsunami also caused more than $310 million in property damage.

The powerful tsunami was not finished. It moved across the Pacific Ocean at 400 miles (644 km) per hour. At midnight it hit the beach at Depoe, Oregon, and carried away four children. The next morning, the tsunami reached Crescent City, California. There it killed ten people and destroyed 150 stores.

Tsunamis spread out from an earthquake's epicenter just as small ripples move across a pond when a rock is thrown into the water.

This photo shows Kodiak Island, Alaska, after the deadly 1964 tsunami.

They travel in circles that grow wider and wider until they eventually reach the shore. This pattern sometimes allows one tsunami to strike two or three different regions of the world.

TSUNAMI SIZE

The shape of a tsunami changes greatly as it moves through the ocean. The strongest surge is underwater, close to the ocean floor. The waves of a tsunami at the ocean's surface may not be very tall. A tsunami even can pass beneath a ship and not be felt by the crew. As the tsunami approaches land, however, the ocean floor gets shallower. The shallow floor slows down the tsunami at its base. The floor also pushes the waves upward. Meanwhile, more waves keep coming from behind. They push into the front waves. The rear waves become larger than the front waves. The swells get closer and closer together until, eventually, they merge into one giant wave. A two-foot (61-cm) swell can turn into an 80-foot (24-m) wave as a tsunami approaches land.

Wavelength

The distance between two waves is called the wavelength. The wavelength of a tsunami is very different from that of other waves, such as tidal waves. Most ocean waves have wave-lengths ranging from 30 to 60 feet (9 to 18 m).

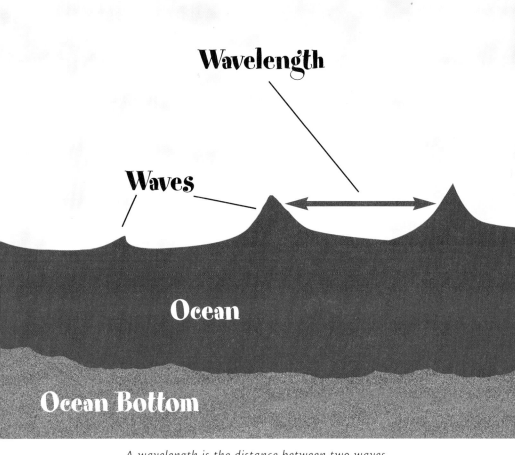

A wavelength is the distance between two waves.

The waves in a tsunami can be as far apart as 300 miles (483 km)! A 300-mile wavelength is a definite sign of a tsunami. As the tsunami gets closer to shore, the wavelengths shorten. They get shorter until all of the waves merge to form one giant tsunami wave.

TSUNAMI SPEED

A tsunami's size is not the only thing that changes as it approaches land. The speed of the tsunami changes as well. Tsunamis travel very quickly over the open waters of an ocean. They usually move between 500 to 600 miles per hour (805 to 966 kph). This is as fast as some jets fly! As a tsunami gets closer to land, tsunami waves bunch up and slow down. A tsunami that starts at 600 miles per hour (966 kph) can slow down to less than 100 miles per hour (161 kph). Tsunamis traveling at this speed are still very dangerous because they are so big.

LOCAL MOTION

Tsunamis that start within 100 miles (161 km) of land are called local tsunamis. Local tsunamis are the most dangerous because people have less time to prepare for them. Also, local tsunamis are stronger than regular tsunamis. Local tsunamis hit land soon after they begin.

Waves have less time to spread out and die down. When a local tsunami hits a populated coastline, the property damage and the loss of life can be enormous.

TSUNAMI DANGER

When a tsunami hits, millions of gallons of water surge over the land. A tsunami can move large rocks, boats, cars—and even buildings. People who are used to smaller waves don't realize how strong and fast a tsunami can be. In many cases, people have died as they stayed to watch a tsunami come in from the sea.

Tsunami waters hit so violently that they can kill people on impact. Other people are knocked

DID YOU KNOW?

The last tsunami of the twentieth century happened on November 26, 1999. It was caused by an earthquake in the South Pacific. The tsunami hit several islands, including Hawaii and Fiji.

unconscious and are drowned. The water moves with such force that it can immediately fill a victim's lungs with water. Most tsunami-related deaths are caused by drowning.

Flooding

Tsunami waters can knock apart homes completely. They also can flood office buildings, warehouses, factories, and farmland. A major tsunami will cause more damage to buildings than will an earthquake.

During a 1993 tsunami in Japan, water inland reached as high as 100 feet (30.5 m)—as tall as a ten-story building! On the Japanese island of Okushiri, a tsunami washed away half of the island's 690 homes. All wooden structures were totally destroyed. Power lines were destroyed along several miles of Okushiri's western shore. Concrete roads were washed away and the pieces ended up several miles inland.

A 1993 tsunami that hit Japan destroyed much of the coastline.

Dragged Out to Sea

People who are lucky enough to survive the initial hit of a tsunami still face the threat of drowning. If you have ever been to the seashore, you know that ocean waves flow onto the beach and then ebb (recede). A tsunami works in the same way, but it is a giant wave. First, it breaks violently on the shore, attacking the land. Then, it ebbs back into the sea. Survivors of the tsunami's impact can still be sucked into the sea and drowned.

DIRTY WATER

You might think that a tsunami's sudden surge of water would clean the land. The opposite is true. Tsunami water is usually very dirty. As the water rushes toward land, it picks up all kinds of things, such as rocks, mud, wood, and sealife (both alive and dead). When the tsunami water recedes, it leaves behind those things to litter the land.

The flooding that occurs after a tsunami hits also creates dirty conditions. If a tsunami hits a populated coastal area, it is likely to unearth places where chemicals and sewage are stored. The water that remains after a tsunami recedes probably will be polluted. People who survive the tsunami can become sick if they come in contact with polluted water. Survivors that have cuts on their skin can get infections.

The water left standing after a 1999 tsunami in Turkey was extremely polluted.

CHAPTER THREE

PREDICTION AND SAFETY TIPS

Two earthquakes struck just off the northeast shore of Papua New Guinea on July 17, 1998. The earthquakes produced a local tsunami that surged toward the island nation. The water was 30 feet (9 m) high as it crossed over the beach. Thousands of stunned villagers were crushed by the violent waves. Many people were dragged out to sea and were drowned. One official said: "Papua New Guinea has no warning system, but even if it did, it wouldn't have mattered. The earthquake was so close to land, people didn't even have time to run."

The coastline where the tsunami hit had been home to about 10,000 people. After the devastation, local authorities confirmed that 1,600 people were dead. More than 3,000 others were reported missing or were otherwise unaccounted for.

In 1998, a tsunami struck Papua New Guinea, killing thousands of people.

This special buoy is placed in the ocean to serve as an early warning device in the event of a tsunami.

In 1946, a tsunami hit Alaska and Hawaii, killing a total of 164 people. After this disaster, scientists tried to figure out how to predict tsunami disasters. Scientists established the Pacific Tsunami Warning Center (PTWC) in Honolulu, Hawaii. Honolulu is close to the center of the Pacific Ocean, where most tsunamis occur. From its Honolulu location, the PTWC uses state-of-the-art computers and satellites to watch over the Pacific Ocean twenty-four hours a day, year-round.

There also is a smaller center for tsunami detection in Palmer, Alaska. After the 1964 tsunami in Prince William Sound, local officials were convinced that they needed to take action. They formed the U.S. West Coast and Alaska Warning Center in 1967. Both the PTWC and the center in Palmer have helped people living near the Pacific Ocean to prepare for oncoming tsunamis.

SEISMOGRAPH

The most important tool in detecting tsunamis is the seismograph. A seismograph measures and records the shock waves given off by an earthquake. Because 95 percent of tsunamis are caused by earthquakes, the seismograph is a good tool to predict tsunamis. Seismic waves travel faster than do tsunami waves, so when a seismograph picks up strong readings, scientists have time to study the data and find the earthquake's epicenter.

Scientists use the seismograph readings to grade the magnitude (strength) of an earthquake. A quake's magnitude is graded on a scale of 0 to 10. Most tsunamis are caused by earthquakes that have a magnitude of 7.5 or greater. To be safe, officials issue a tsunami warning for every earthquake that has a magnitude of 6.5 or greater. They issue a warning to everyone within three hours' travel time (based on wave speed) from the quake's epicenter. The states of Alaska, California, Hawaii, Oregon, and Washington have seismic warning centers.

Although seismograph readings can help to predict some tsunamis, they are not useful in predicting local tsunamis. It is impossible to warn people about local tsunamis. Local tsunami waves reach land too quickly.

SATELLITES

Some satellites that orbit (circle) Earth in space have instruments that can read the height of the ocean. These instruments are called radar altimeters. Radar altimeters can indicate when tsunami waves start to build up in the ocean.

PRESSURE DETECTORS

Special devices on the ocean floor can sense when pressure builds up in the surrounding water. These devices are called pressure detectors. If a pressure increase occurs, the detector sends a sound-wave signal to a surface buoy. The buoy then transmits this signal to a satellite. The satellite signals a tsunami warning center on land.

SEAWALLS

In Japan, some coastal areas are protected by seawalls. Seawalls are metal or cement barriers that are built between coastal towns and the sea. Seawalls can work against small- or medium-size tsunamis to prevent flooding. However, some tsunamis become so big that they wash right over the seawalls.

SAFETY TIPS

If you live near the ocean or if you ever visit the beach, it is important to know what precautions to take in case of a tsunami.

- Know the height above sea level of your street and the distance of your street from the coast. Officials may call for people to evacuate (leave an area). They may do so based on an area's height above sea level or on its distance from the coastline.
- Pick an inland location that is high above sea level. Know how to get there quickly in

This seawall was built in Nagasaki, Japan, to protect against tsunami waves.

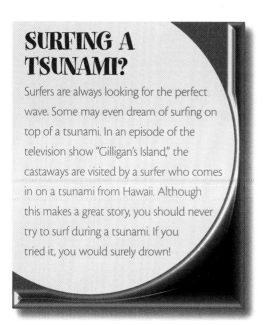

SURFING A TSUNAMI?

Surfers are always looking for the perfect wave. Some may even dream of surfing on top of a tsunami. In an episode of the television show "Gilligan's Island," the castaways are visited by a surfer who comes in on a tsunami from Hawaii. Although this makes a great story, you should never try to surf during a tsunami. If you tried it, you would surely drown!

case of a tsunami or a tsunami warning.

• Have an emergency kit ready in case you have to evacuate. Your kit should include batteries, a first aid kit, a flashlight, food, medicine, a portable radio, sturdy shoes, and water.

• If you hear an official tsunami warning on the radio or on television, leave the area at once. Tsunami warnings are issued when officials are certain that a tsunami threat exists.

• Return home only after authorities say it is safe to do so.

Be prepared if a tsunami should strike your area.

Fact Sheet · · · · · · · ·

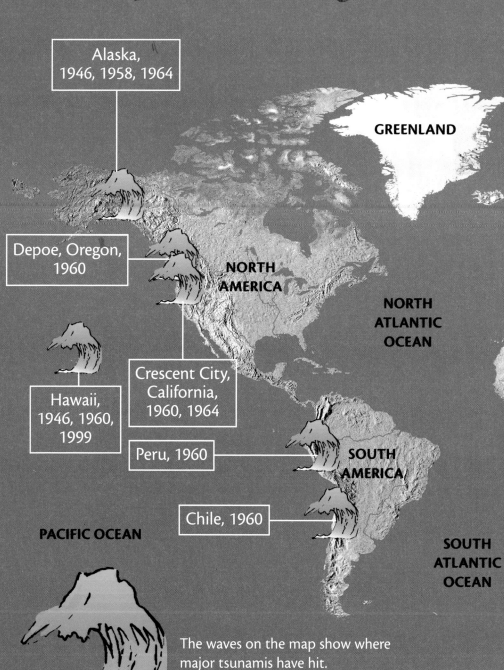

Alaska,
1946, 1958, 1964

GREENLAND

Depoe, Oregon,
1960

NORTH
AMERICA

NORTH
ATLANTIC
OCEAN

Crescent City,
California,
1960, 1964

Hawaii,
1946, 1960,
1999

Peru, 1960

SOUTH
AMERICA

Chile, 1960

PACIFIC OCEAN

SOUTH
ATLANTIC
OCEAN

The waves on the map show where
major tsunamis have hit.

Major Tsunamis

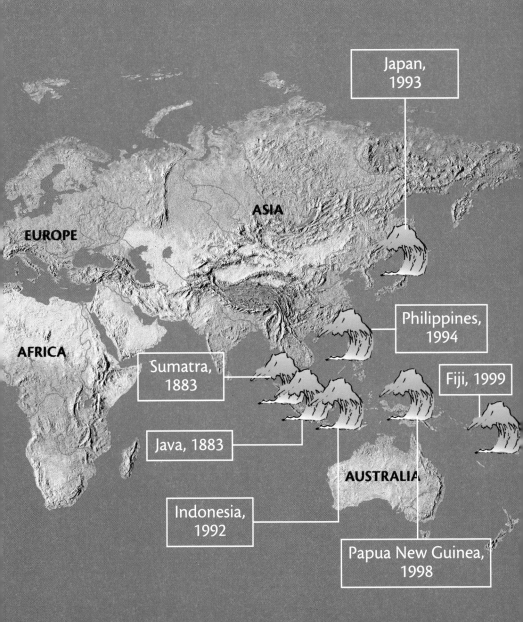

Japan,
1993

ASIA

EUROPE

Philippines,
1994

AFRICA

Sumatra,
1883

Fiji, 1999

Java, 1883

Indonesia,
1992

AUSTRALIA

Papua New Guinea,
1998

crust the topmost layer of Earth, made of solid rock

earthquake when shock waves cause the ground to vibrate

ebb when ocean waves recede

epicenter the starting point of an earthquake

eruption when a volcano explodes

evacuate to leave an area

gravity the force that pulls matter toward the center of Earth

landslide huge rocks or large chunks of land that slide down mountains or hills

magma hot, liquid rock from deep in the Earth

magnitude size and intensity

orbit to circle

pressure detectors devices that can sense when pressure builds up in water

radar altimeters instruments that can read the height of an ocean

Ring of Fire a circle of active underwater volcanoes that surrounds the Pacific Ocean

satellite a machine that orbits Earth

NEW WORDS

seawalls barriers built between a coastal town and the sea

seismic sea waves another name for tsunami waves

seismic (shock) waves shock waves that travel outward from the epicenter of an earthquake

seismograph the instrument used to record the vibrations of an earthquake

swell a large surge

tectonic plates slabs of rock that make up Earth's crust

tidal wave a tall wave caused by ocean tides

tsunami a sea wave caused by movement in the ocean

volcano an opening in Earth's crust where magma and hot gas come to the surface

wavelength the space between waves

FOR FURTHER READING

Drohan, Michele I. *Tsunamis*. New York: The Rosen Publishing Group, 1999.

Flaherty, Michael. *Tidal Waves and Flooding*. Brookfield, CT: Millbrook Press, 1998.

Klutz Press. *Disaster Science*. Palo Alto, CA: Klutz Press, 1998.

Souza, D. M. *Powerful Waves*. Minneapolis: The Lerner Publishing Group, 1992.

RESOURCES

Pacific Tsunami Museum
P.O. Box 806
Hilo, HI 96721
Web site: *www.tsunami.org*
This museum educates the public about the dangers of tsunamis. It also serves as a memorial to people that have lost their lives to tsunamis.

Tsunami!
Web site: *www.geophys.washington.edu/tsunami*
This site contains information about recent tsunamis. You can learn about the impact that tsunamis have, and the best ways to survive them.

TSUNAMI!
Web site: *www.sciam.com/1999/0599issue/0599gonzalez.html*
Read about deadly tsunamis and a new way to track these killer waves.

Tsunami Research Program
Web site: *www.pmel.noaa.gov/tsunami/*
On this government site, you can learn more about tsunamis and the dangers associated with these giant waves. The site has interesting facts about tsunamis, information about tsunami warning systems, and links to other tsunami sites.

INDEX

INDEX

ABOUT THE AUTHOR

Luke Thompson was born in Delaware. He holds a degree in English literature from James Madison University. He lives in Vail, Colorado.